Simple strategies to boost your online presence
[that every company should apply]

Copyright © 2024 Reginaldo Osnildo

I0427345

PRESENTATION

INTRODUCTION TO DIGITAL MARKETING: AN EASY-TO-UNDERSTAND OVERVIEW OF WHAT DIGITAL MARKETING IS AND WHY IT'S ESSENTIAL FOR LOCAL BUSINESS

TARGET AUDIENCE IDENTIFICATION: HOW TO UNDERSTAND WHO YOUR CUSTOMERS ARE AND WHAT THEY ARE LOOKING FOR ONLINE

BASIC CONTENT MARKETING: TIPS FOR CREATING RELEVANT CONTENT THAT ATTRACTS AND ENGAGES YOUR AUDIENCE

EFFICIENT USE OF SOCIAL MEDIA: SIMPLE STRATEGIES FOR USING PLATFORMS LIKE FACEBOOK AND INSTAGRAM TO PROMOTE YOUR BUSINESS

BASIC SEO FOR BEGINNERS: SEO BASICS TO IMPROVE YOUR SITE'S VISIBILITY IN SEARCH ENGINES

EMAIL MARKETING FOR SMALL BUSINESS: HOW TO START EFFECTIVE AND EASY TO MANAGE EMAIL MARKETING CAMPAIGNS

SIMPLE DATA ANALYSIS: UNDERSTANDING AND USING BASIC DATA TO IMPROVE YOUR ONLINE PRESENCE

AFFORDABLE ONLINE ADVERTISING: INTRODUCTION TO DIGITAL ADVERTISING AND HOW TO GET STARTED ON A LIMITED BUDGET

RESPONDING TO REVIEWS AND ONLINE REPUTATION MANAGEMENT: HOW TO MANAGE THE REPUTATION OF YOUR ONLINE BUSINESS AND RESPOND TO COMMENTS AND REVIEWS

ACTION PLAN AND SUCCESS MEASURES: DEFINING CLEAR AND MEASURABLE GOALS AND HOW TO EVALUATE THE SUCCESS OF YOUR ONLINE STRATEGIES.

CONCLUSION AND MAP FOR APPLYING THE STRATEGIES LEARNED IN THE NEXT 90 DAYS, STARTING FROM TODAY: A DAY BY STEP STEP BY DAY FOR ENTREPRENEURS TO APPLY SIMPLE STRATEGIES

REGINALDO OSNILDO

PRESENTATION

Welcome to the book **"Simple strategies to boost your online presence [that every company should apply]**"! If you own or manage a small or medium-sized company (SME), this book was written with you in mind and the challenges of promoting your business online.

We know that managing a company already demands a lot of your time, that's why we've prepared this practical and objective guide, focused on proven strategies that really work and that you can apply without complications.

Over the next chapters, you will learn essential digital marketing notions and discover simple and affordable ways to increase your business's online presence. We range from identifying your target audience and creating attractive content on social media, to improving search engine positioning, starting email marketing campaigns and much more.

The idea is to provide a complete, yet simplified, introduction to the world of digital marketing, highlighting only what is truly essential for small businesses, like yours, to stand out online. You will leave this book ready to put the main strategies into practice and start reaping the rewards of a solid digital presence.

And don't worry if you start from scratch in terms of digital marketing knowledge. We think about all the important details and explain each concept clearly and objectively, using simple language and practical examples.

Below is a summary of what you will find in each chapter:

- **Chapter 1 - Introduction to digital marketing:** understand what digital marketing is, its importance today and why investing in it is essential to attract more customers.

- **Chapter 2 - Target audience identification:** learn how to define your target audience to direct your online actions and content.

- Chapter 3 - Basic content marketing: see how to produce relevant content on social media to engage your audience.

- Chapter 4 - Efficient use of social media: learn about the main social networks and how to use them to your advantage to promote your brand and products.

And so on, covering all fundamental strategies such as SEO, email marketing, online advertising, reputation management, goal setting and measuring results.

In the last chapter, you will find a detailed action plan, with a step-by-step guide to applying everything you learned over 90 days. It's your launch pad to take off online!

As you read further, we invite you to put the tips presented into practice. We want this book to be a living guide, which you can consult and follow to the letter to see concrete results in your business.

Get ready to boost your online presence!

We hope you find a lot of value in these pages. Happy reading and much success! Let's move on together to the next chapter.

Yours sincerely,

Reginaldo Osnildo

INTRODUCTION TO DIGITAL MARKETING: AN EASY-TO-UNDERSTAND OVERVIEW OF WHAT DIGITAL MARKETING IS AND WHY IT'S ESSENTIAL FOR LOCAL BUSINESS

This chapter aims to provide a simple, introductory overview of what digital marketing is and why it is so important for local businesses like yours.

Let's start by explaining what this expression that is so often used when we talk about strategies for promoting brands and products on the internet means: digital marketing.

Marketing refers to all actions to promote brands, products and services. Marketing strategies allow local businesses, such as your SME, to connect with potential customers through offline advertisements (magazines, newspapers, pamphlets, radio, etc.).

And that is exactly why digital marketing strategies have become indispensable for anyone who wants to grow their business nowadays. More and more consumers are researching, comparing options and even making purchases 100% online.

According to recent data in Brazil:

- 72% of consumers research online before purchasing in physical stores ;

- 64% of people trust online reviews from other buyers more than traditional advertisements ;

- 52% of consumers do local searches on their smartphone to find stores, products or services near their location .

So it's clear that if your SME isn't finding these consumers during online searches, many sales are being lost.

And a solid presence in digital media goes far beyond having a website or Facebook page. It is necessary to implement well-planned digital marketing strategies to really attract the attention of these potential customers and stand out from the competition.

EXPLAINING THE IMPORTANCE OF DIGITAL MARKETING

Digital marketing refers to all marketing strategies and techniques applied in digital media, such as websites, social media, search engines and other online channels. The main objective is to promote your brand and connect your business to the public through the digital environment.

In other words, while traditional marketing focuses on offline advertisements (magazines, newspapers, pamphlets, radio, etc.), digital marketing focuses its efforts on online spaces and platforms.

And why is this so important today? Simple: because your audience is on the internet!

People are spending more and more time online, whether looking for products and services, consuming content, interacting on social media or finding out about news. Ignoring this behavior means leaving your business off the radar of potential new customers.

Furthermore, digital marketing has many unique advantages compared to traditional approaches, such as:

- Lower cost to reach more people

- Measurement of results in real time

- Precise segmentation of target audiences

- Greater control over your communication

- Personalization of user experience

- Process automation

For an SME looking to expand its sales and reach new local customers, it is more than proven that establishing an online presence through digital marketing strategies is absolutely fundamental these days. There's no way around it: your business needs to enter the digital environment!

BENEFITS OF DIGITAL MARKETING FOR SMALL BUSINESSES

Maybe you're still not 100% convinced that it's worth investing time and resources in digital marketing. But consider these proven positive impacts:

- **Increase in the reach of your brand:** through the online environment you can expose your brand and products to many more people, expanding business possibilities.

- **Better local visibility:** inhabitants and potential customers in your region seek local business information online, so it is crucial to have a presence digitally.

- **More engagement with your audience:** you can interact directly with customers and followers through social media, bringing your brand closer and generating stronger relationships.

- **Sales 24 hours a day:** your online store or digital channels work uninterruptedly, receiving orders and selling even when your physical store is already closed.

- **Modernization of your brand:** demonstrating that you also use online channels conveys an image of modernity and update that attracts new customers.

- **Savings and optimization:** several digital marketing strategies can be implemented with low investment and help reduce costs in other areas.

I hope I convinced you about the importance of digital marketing in highlighting small local businesses today!

On the next pages we will go into more detail, teaching you the basics so you can take your first steps with digital strategies.

Don't forget to also follow our next chapters, where we will present the best tactics and tools for you to easily apply digital marketing to your business and boost your online presence.

In the next chapter we will dive into understanding the target audience, which is the basis of any marketing strategy, whether digital or traditional. But you can take the next crucial step now, which is to evaluate your current online presence and your most urgent needs.

TARGET AUDIENCE IDENTIFICATION: HOW TO UNDERSTAND WHO YOUR CUSTOMERS ARE AND WHAT THEY ARE LOOKING FOR ONLINE

Now that you know the basic principles behind digital marketing, it's time to get your hands dirty and start designing your personalized strategies. And the most important element to direct your actions is to deeply understand who your target audience is.

In this chapter, I will guide you step by step through the entire process of identifying your ideal customers and analyzing how they behave online. With this information in hand, you'll be ready to target your digital marketing efforts specifically to attract more of this audience and get your business off the ground!

WHAT IS TARGET AUDIENCE?

First of all, we need to understand the concept of target audience (or persona, as it is also called). The target audience represents a specific group of people who are most likely to be interested in your product or service.

Therefore, it is a mistake to want to sell to "all types" of people. This makes your marketing initiatives too generic. The ideal is to direct your communication and efforts to impact a well-defined group with common characteristics and interests.

But how can we better define and understand this audience? There are well-established techniques for this, which we will cover in the next sections.

CREATING BUYER PERSONAS

A buyer persona is a semi-fictional profile that represents your ideal customers. To create them, you first need to gather as much information as possible about your real customers, such as:

- Demographic data (age, sex, marital status, family income, educational level, type of housing, etc.)

- Geographic location (country, state, city)

- Behaviors and habits (what do they like to do in their free time?)

- Pains and needs (what problems do you want to solve when buying your product?)

- Objections or impediments to purchase

The idea is to draw very detailed sociodemographic profiles and deeply understand the interests, values and motivations behind the purchasing decisions of these personas.

Some personas may end up being very similar. Others may represent completely different target audiences. The ideal is to create between 2 and 4 personas for your business.

You can define fictitious names, ages, representative photos and even short first-person descriptions to personify each profile. This helps your team always keep these personas in mind as your ideal customers.

ANALYZING YOUR DIGITAL BEHAVIOR

Now let's understand how your target audience behaves online. Where do they browse the internet? What search terms do they use? What content do they consume?

You can discover these answers by analyzing:

- Where does your website traffic come from

- What terms people use to reach your website

- What your audience comments and shares on social media

- What websites and blogs do they frequent?

- Competitor pages that attract your target audience

Test it yourself by searching on Google and social media using keywords that your audience would use. See which are the main websites displayed and the most used content formats (videos, texts, etc.).

Analytical tools like Google Analytics also provide valuable information about geolocation, age, gender and the paths your visitors take through your website.

All of these tips will help you map out the main online touchpoints with your target audience. This will make it easier to attract them with relevant content.

FUNCTIONING YOUR FOCUS

As you get to know your ideal customers, certain profiles tend to stand out because they already buy more from you today or because they have great potential in the future.

For example, if you have a pet store, you may notice that 73% of your sales come from women, aged 30 to 50, married and with children. In other words, this could be your main buyer persona right now.

Don't be afraid to focus much of your marketing efforts on this most profitable audience. They have already shown interest and are your priority to expand sales quickly.

Keep your buyer personas up to date! New consumers with different profiles may emerge and you need to be prepared to adjust your strategies accordingly.

I hope you now have a good understanding of your target audience and how they behave on digital media. This information will set the right direction for all of our upcoming digital marketing initiatives.

In the next chapter, I'll teach you simple content marketing concepts to create posts and materials that truly attract your target audiences, engage, and convert visitors into customers!

BASIC CONTENT MARKETING: TIPS FOR CREATING RELEVANT CONTENT THAT ATTRACTS AND ENGAGES YOUR AUDIENCE

Now that we know our target audience well and where to find them online, it's time to start attracting them!

And the most effective way to grab anyone's attention and generate interest these days is through relevant and engaging content.

Therefore, in this chapter I will present everything you need to know about content marketing to start producing incredible materials for your audience.

WHAT IS CONTENT MARKETING?

Content marketing refers to any type of digital media (text, video, audio, infographics, e-books, etc.) that a brand creates and distributes online with the aim of not just selling, but educating, informing and engaging your target audience.

In other words, it is a type of approach focused on attracting the right people by delivering extremely useful, relevant and interesting content to them.

Instead of constantly promoting your products or carrying out aggressive advertising, the idea is to first gain the public's trust and sympathy, establishing your company as a reliable source of information in that niche.

But why does this strategy work so well?

BENEFITS OF CONTENT MARKETING

Some of the main benefits of content marketing are:

- Attract more qualified visitors to your website

- Reduce the need to invest in paid ads

- Increase conversion rates into sales

- Improve the perception of your brand and products

- Position your company as an authority in the segment

- Outperform the competition by offering more value to the consumer

In other words, investing in quality content is a proven efficient strategy with a great return on investment for gaining new customers.

Now that you know the importance of producing content, let's look at tips for creating incredible materials.

CHOOSING CONTENT FORMATS

There are a multitude of formats you can use to produce content, such as:

- Blog articles

- Videos

- Podcasts

- E-books

- Infographics

- Lists and guides

- Case studies

- Researches

- Webinars

Analyze the formats that your target audience consumes most and start there. A good tip is also to vary between formats, bringing new content in video, audio and texts.

This keeps your audience interested!

DEFINING THEMES AND TITLES THAT ATTRACT

Now that you know which formats you want to work with, it's time to determine what you're going to talk about in this content.

Always remember the interests, needs and pains of your target audience. What type of content would really deliver value to them?

Some ideas are:

- Solutions to common problems

- Savings and cost reduction tips

- How to make or use your product

- Mistakes to avoid

- Trends and news in the sector

- Curious surveys and statistics

- Successful case studies

- Lists with top 5, 10 or 15 something

- Step by step guides

For titles, use engaging sentences with the structure "How to do X", "The definitive guide to X", "The best X".

WIDE DISCLOSURE

Finally, there's no point in creating amazing content if no one has access to it. You need to amplify distribution, using all possible channels:

- Your website and blog

- Social media

- E-mail marketing

- Messaging apps

- Paid media to boost posts

- Partnerships with other websites and influencers

The greater the reach of your message, the more successful it will be and the more audience you will attract.

Well, I hope you are now inspired with lots of ideas and ready to start producing amazing content for your audience!

In the next chapter, I will teach you powerful strategies to further leverage your presence on social media. Don't miss it!

EFFICIENT USE OF SOCIAL MEDIA: SIMPLE STRATEGIES FOR USING PLATFORMS LIKE FACEBOOK AND INSTAGRAM TO PROMOTE YOUR BUSINESS

At this point, you already know the basics about digital marketing and content marketing. Now it's time to dive into one of the most important areas with the greatest potential for small businesses: social media!

In this chapter, I will teach you everything you need to do to efficiently and cost-effectively use the main social platforms - especially Facebook and Instagram - in order to promote your brand and boost your sales.

THE IMPORTANCE OF SOCIAL MEDIA TODAY

It's no news to anyone that platforms like Facebook, Instagram and YouTube completely dominate people's attention on the internet nowadays. These are apps that we have the habit of checking dozens of times a day, both on our cell phones and on our computers.

And for local brands, being where your audience spends so much time is a unique opportunity to gain visibility, interact with potential customers and generate recognition for your brand with minimal costs.

But just creating a social media profile is not enough. You need to know how to use them to your advantage to really attract engaged followers and generate sales.

In the next sections, we'll focus on everything that needs to be done on Facebook and Instagram, which are currently two of the main social showcases for local businesses to stand out.

OPTIMIZING YOUR FACEBOOK PROFILE AND PAGE

First, if you don't already have an official page for your company on Facebook, hurry up and create one! In addition to your professional page, it is also recommended to keep your personal profile active on the platform, interacting with local groups and promoting your business.

Then, invest the time to fully optimize your business page:

- Choose a standardized cover photo for your brand

- Post eye-catching photos and videos about your products/ services

- Fill in all description information, address, website, etc.

- Clearly define "Contact Us" and "Buy" action buttons

- Create and actively manage the post feed

Also remember to interact with page visitors, responding to all messages and comments. This conveys an image of closeness to the public.

ATTRACTING QUALIFIED FOLLOWERS

Now is the time to start gaining reach and followers. Some of the best strategies are:

- Invest in paid ads targeted at your target audience

- Make periodic publications with relevant content

- Use local and thematic hashtags to increase reach

- Promote sweepstakes and giveaways to gain likes and followers

- Sponsor posts with influential profiles in your region

- Create events and invite members from local groups

The goal is to bring as many people as possible to your page who are truly interested in the type of content and products you offer.

LEVERAGING SALES ON INSTAGRAM

Instagram has immense potential to really sell your brand and products in a visual and creative way. It is the ideal network for businesses that work with fashion, gastronomy, travel, interior design or selling any photogenic item.

The ideal strategy involves three pillars:

- Clean and standardized feed:

Have a unique visual line in your photos, using the same filters, similar compositions and colors of your brand.

- Highlights with products/services:

In Stories and highlights, present your items for sale in an attractive way, showing the products in use.

- Direct link to purchase:

Leave a direct link to your website or sales WhatsApp in your profile bio, inviting people to buy after they become interested in your publications.

These are just some basic ideas on how to make the most of the main social networks to promote a local brand.

There are many more strategies and features that we can explore on these powerful platforms. But now you can start working.

In the next chapter, I will talk about a fundamental concept for improving the organic reach of your website and online business: SEO.

BASIC SEO FOR BEGINNERS: SEO BASICS TO IMPROVE YOUR SITE'S VISIBILITY IN SEARCH ENGINES

Now that we've seen the power of social media, it's time to focus on another important front to improve your company's online visibility: SEO, or Search engine Optimization.

In a nutshell, SEO means search engine optimization and involves a set of techniques to improve your website's positioning in Google results and other search engines.

Therefore, mastering basic SEO concepts is essential to attract more qualified visitors and customers through organic searches, without having to invest anything in ads.

In this chapter, I will present introductory but essential notions of SEO that you need to start applying now to make your website more visible and authoritative on the internet.

Shall we start this journey?

UNDERSTANDING SEO

As we said, SEO means Search engine Optimization, or Search Engine Optimization in Portuguese. The goal of SEO is to improve different aspects of a website so that it appears as high as possible in organic (non-paid) search engine results.

In other words, when someone types a keyword related to your niche into Google, you want your website to appear in the first results, even on the first page.

This is because being among the first organic results brings some clear advantages:

- Many more people click and visit your website

- Conveys authority and relevance of your brand

- Reduces the need for paid advertisements

- Attracts more qualified visitors with purchasing intent

- Improves local visibility of your offline business

Therefore, if you truly want to increase your online presence and attract new visitors and sales, you cannot ignore SEO. Let's look at some simple yet powerful tips to improve your results.

SEO TIPS FOR BEGINNERS

Start applying these 5 basic SEO techniques now:

- **Research the best keywords:** Determine exactly what terms and phrases people search for for the products/services you offer and focus on those words, incorporating them into your content.

- **Optimize website pages and texts:** Include organically searched keywords in the title, URL and text of each page on your website. This will show Google what that page is about.

- **Improve the mobile experience:** Most searches today come from smartphones. Therefore, your website needs to be fast, lightweight and easy to navigate on these devices.

- **Increase authority with external links:** Get backlinks from other websites related to your website's content. This helps Google understand that you are an authority on that specific topic.

- **Analyze Google Analytics data:** See which keywords already bring visitors to your pages and browsing behaviors on the site. Then, focus on optimizing these areas even further.

That's the basics. As you master SEO, you can move on to more advanced techniques.

FREE SEO TOOLS

To put SEO into practice in a simplified way, some tools I recommend are:

- Google Keyword Planner: to research new keywords

- Google Analytics: to analyze data from your website

- Google PageSpeed Insights: shows the website's mobile experience

- MozBar or SEMRush : technically evaluates a page

- Yoast SEO: SEO plugin for WordPress

Then that's it! Start by applying these initial optimization tips to your website's texts and pages to climb the rankings and attract more traffic and sales through organic search.

In the next chapter, I will teach you about an important lead nurturing and sales automation strategy: email marketing!

EMAIL MARKETING FOR SMALL BUSINESS: HOW TO START EFFECTIVE AND EASY TO MANAGE EMAIL MARKETING CAMPAIGNS

In the last few lessons, you saw different ways to reach more people online and generate authority for your business through content, SEO and social media.

Now it's time to learn a powerful lead nurturing and continuous sales strategy, essential for every small business: email marketing!

In this chapter, I'll show you how to easily create and manage effective email campaigns to sell your products 24/7.

WHAT IS EMAIL MARKETING?

E-mail marketing consists of the automated or scheduled sending of relevant commercial communications to a specific base of contacts interested in your business.

In other words, after collecting emails from leads and customers, you can continue nurturing this relationship by periodically sending:

- Promotions

- New products

- Content tips

- Events

- Webinars and more

In addition to generating ongoing sales, this approach helps build loyalty with your brand and reduce marketing costs. After all, advertising via email is much cheaper and more practical than via traditional mail or advertisements.

EMAIL MARKETING TOOLS

To start your campaigns, you first need to choose a good email marketing tool. Some popular and easy-to-use options are:

-MailChimp

- SendinBlue

- ActiveCampaign

These platforms have ready-made professional email templates that you can customize with your content and visual identity. In addition, they have features such as analytics, flow automation and integrations with CRMs.

You don't need to limit yourself to the examples I brought, most have a free or very affordable plan for small businesses, which makes them very attractive for entrepreneurs who want to start with email marketing without high investments.

BUILDING YOUR CONTACT LIST

Now it's time to collect those precious customer and lead emails! Some simple ways to get interested contacts are:

- Offer discount coupon in exchange for email

- Create digital magnets on your website with free content (e-book, video lesson, checklist...) in exchange for contact

- Advertise on social media and Stories inviting people to your list

- Create specific versions of landing pages with forms to capture leads

Always fully respect the LGPD and be completely transparent about what you will do with the data you collect, giving people the option to cancel at any time. This is fundamental!

Also remember to segment your list, separating current customers from potential new customers. This way, you can better personalize your communications.

CREATING EFFECTIVE CAMPAIGNS

Finally, when creating your campaigns, bet on emails:

- Short and direct, always to the point (max 200 words)

- With responsive design (easy to read on mobile)

- With clear calls to action (Buy now / Learn more)

- With images and little text

- With personal data and interest targeting

- With monitored performance indicators

Additionally, test different sending days and times to find out what works best for your audience in terms of openings and clicks.

Well, I hope you are now confident to kickstart email marketing for your business. It is an excellent cost-benefit strategy that cannot be missed in your digital presence.

In the next chapter, we will learn about low-cost strategies to boost your online presence through ads.

SIMPLE DATA ANALYSIS: UNDERSTANDING AND USING BASIC DATA TO IMPROVE YOUR ONLINE PRESENCE

So far we have seen several digital marketing strategies to increase the reach and sales of your business. But how do you know if all these tactics are actually working or not?

The answer lies in data analysis!

In this chapter, I will show you in a simple and practical way how to interpret and use essential metrics and insights to understand what is going right or wrong in your online presence. With this information in hand, it becomes much easier to make assertive decisions.

Let's understand more about data analysis?

THE IMPORTANCE OF BEING DATA-DRIVEN

In a nutshell, being data- driven means making your business decisions based on data and facts, not just guesswork and hunches.

This is especially important in the online world, where there are endless possibilities of things to try and optimize to improve results.

Some benefits of adopting a data-driven mindset are:

- Reduce risks in marketing choices

- Identify the paths that really lead to conversions

- Eliminate initiatives that do not deliver results

- Better understand your audience and market

- Underpin everything you do with solid insights

Therefore, there cannot be a lack of a routine for monitoring key metrics, setting goals and making decisions based on the numbers they provide.

ESSENTIAL ANALYSIS TOOLS

To start extracting this valuable information, some tools you need to connect to your website and online channels are:

- **Google Analytics:** The most popular web analytics solution in the world. Offers complete data on visitor behavior on your website.

- **Facebook Analytics:** Engagement metrics and reach of your publications and ads on the social network.

- **Google Search Console:** Insights into organic queries that bring people to your website and content.

- **Email marketing tools:** Data on openings, clicks and conversions in your campaigns.

Dashboards like Google Data Studio also help consolidate data from multiple sources into easy-to-follow visual dashboards.

ESSENTIAL METRICS AND KPIS

Analyzing every possible number will just overwhelm you. Therefore, focus on the really decisive metrics. Some essential KPIs are:

- Sessions and users on the website

- Page views

- Bounce rate and time on site

- Traffic sources (organic, social, direct...)

- Sales conversion rate

- Number of leads captured

- Reach on social media

- Engagement (likes, shares, mentions...)

- Return on investment

Pull these crucial indicators for all your digital initiatives and you'll have a very solid 360 view of your efforts.

QUESTIONS THAT DATA ANSWERS

In addition to looking at numbers in isolation, know how to ask them powerful questions, such as:

- Which source generates the most sales for my business?

- Which search terms attract the most qualified visitors?

- Which social network has the best engagement with my audience?

- Which posts/products perform best organically?

- What is the ROI of my online ads?

This continuous questioning will help you make the best decisions based on what really works.

Well, I hope you now realize how vital it is to analyze simple data regularly to understand your online presence and increasingly improve your initiatives.

In the next chapter, I'll talk about how to boost all of this with affordable digital advertising even on a small budget.

AFFORDABLE ONLINE ADVERTISING: INTRODUCTION TO DIGITAL ADVERTISING AND HOW TO GET STARTED ON A LIMITED BUDGET

After deeply understanding your target audience and working on your organic online presence, it's time to accelerate all of this with an extra boost of advertising.

In this chapter, I will provide an introduction to the world of digital advertising, highlighting affordable options for small businesses that want to amplify their reach and traffic quickly, even with a limited budget.

WHAT IS DIGITAL ADVERTISING?

Digital advertising or online advertising refers to all paid advertising formats served on the internet with the purpose of promoting brands, products, services and attracting more sales or leads.

Some popular examples are Google sponsored links and banners, Facebook and Instagram ads, pop-ups on targeted websites, native advertising on blogs, etc.

This is an already consolidated market, which generates tens of billions in investments per year in Brazil alone. And it's no surprise: for small local businesses with a limited budget, starting with digital advertising is simpler and cheaper than using traditional channels, allowing for great returns.

Furthermore, there are now a multitude of digital advertising platforms and formats for you to test and scale little by little, finding exactly what works for your business.

In the next section, I will cover some of them, ideal for small advertisers.

ONLINE ADVERTISING OPTIONS IN ACCOUNT

Check out different accessible channels for you to start your journey with digital ads:

- **Google Ads:** Google's sponsored links system. Focus on words that are very specific to your business to attract only hyper-qualified leads.

- Facebook and Instagram Ads: Advertise to users with your same profile and interests on social networks. Use features like lookalike audiences.

- Native Advertising: Ad formats with a native editorial appearance on targeted websites. Use relevant images and headlines.

- Local influencers: Pay for promotional posts on influencer profiles in your region. Focused and credible.

- Partnerships with blogs: Sponsor posts or make exchanges with websites in your segment: promotion for the sake of promotion.

Tools like Google Trends and Keyword Planner helps you discover the most searched for terms with the least competition, increasing the reach of your money invested in traffic.

Platforms like RD Station are ideal for automating, managing and scaling your campaigns, even without prior technical knowledge.

STRATEGIES FOR CHEAP AND EFFECTIVE ADVERTISING

Here are some golden tips for investing in digital advertising in a smart and economical way:

- Start with a limited budget and time (e.g. R$300/month for 2 months)

- Advertise only to more specific and engaged audiences

- Use geolocation features for people in your region

- Bid low amounts per click to gain share of voice

- Test lots of different content, copy and images

- Monitor results and ROAS in real time

- Immediately pause non-performing ads

- Scale the budget of those that are really efficient

This trial and error process will quickly teach you what really pays off and how to maximize every penny invested to reach other customers online.

And remember: even with small budgets, but very well applied, the results in sales and authority of your brand can be tremendous.

In the next chapter, we will look at good practices for managing your online reputation well.

RESPONDING TO REVIEWS AND ONLINE REPUTATION MANAGEMENT: HOW TO MANAGE THE REPUTATION OF YOUR ONLINE BUSINESS AND RESPOND TO COMMENTS AND REVIEWS

So far you have seen several ways to increase your digital presence, attract more customers and improve your sales. Everything's good!

But equally important is taking good care of your online reputation and image. After all, negative comments or bad reviews can quickly neutralize other marketing efforts.

Therefore, in this chapter we will cover good online reputation management practices and how to deal with feedback, responding appropriately to comments and reviews to cultivate a positive perception of your business.

THE IMPORTANCE OF ONLINE REPUTATION

It's no secret that hundreds of consumers research a company online before purchasing its products or services. And it is precisely through reviews, ratings and mentions that they build an impression about your brand.

TOOLS TO MANAGE YOUR REPUTATION

There are some online solutions that help you track everything that is said about your brand on the internet, such as:

- **Google Alerts:** Receive email updates when your business is mentioned in new content.

- **Google My Business:** monitor and respond to reviews left by customers on local Google searches.

- **Facebook Places :** same case above within Facebook.

- **Reputation sites:** track your aggregate rating on popular review sites such as Brazilian ReclameAQUI , Consumidor.gov.br, etc.

Leave alerts set up so you can be quickly notified when you're tagged in social media posts or receive very negative reviews. The faster you respond, the better!

GOOD PRACTICES WHEN RESPONDING TO REVIEWS

Keep these golden points in mind when communicating with customers online:

- Respond to all public mentions as quickly as possible.

- Be humble, polite and don't get defensive.

- Apologize for the failure or frustration generated.

- Show genuine interest in solving the mentioned problem.

- Offer direct contact options (by phone, email or private chat) to provide support.

- Thank them for their time and feedback.

- Make your answers publicly visible to build authority.

These attitudes go far beyond just putting out fires. They strengthen ties with your customers, turn complainants into fan advocates for your company, and convey professionalism and concern to any new visitor who reads the comments.

PREVENTION IS ALSO THE BEST MEDICINE

Of course, just reacting to negative reviews is not ideal. Also remember that it is cheaper and more efficient to prevent a bad reputation than to cure it.

Some effective preventive strategies are:

- Delight your customers, generating wonderful experiences that they want to share.

- Have quick after-sales communication channels.

- Anticipate complaints by directly answering people's questions.

- Proactively ask good customers for 5-star reviews.

- Build a secure feature where customers can give private feedback before making it public.

The more care and affection you dedicate to your audience, the fewer reputation problems your company will face.

I hope these tips help you cultivate great online reviews and responses that strengthen the credibility that's so important to making your local business stand out online.

In the next chapter, we will see how to set clear objectives and measure the results of your online initiatives

ACTION PLAN AND SUCCESS MEASURES: DEFINING CLEAR AND MEASURABLE GOALS AND HOW TO EVALUATE THE SUCCESS OF YOUR ONLINE STRATEGIES.

At this point, you've already learned the main strategies for increasing your online presence and sales.

Now it's time to ensure that you put all of this into practice in the most structured way possible to truly boost your business.

In this chapter, I will talk about how to draw up a solid action plan with clear objectives, in addition to defining the success metrics that will allow you to monitor the results of digital initiatives.

THE IMPORTANCE OF AN ACTION PLAN

Before tactically executing the strategies taught in this book, it is essential to sit down and build a well-defined action plan that establishes what needs to be done, by whom, within what time frame and with what objective.

This planning is important for a few reasons:

- Avoid getting lost among hundreds of possibilities

- Provides focus on truly essential activities

- Allows you to measure improvement and correct directions

- Involves and aligns everyone on your team

- Maximizes the results of each initiative

Take a few hours to outline all the components of this plan. If it's too difficult at first, get a ready-made digital marketing plan template and customize it with your data. The heavy architectural work will already be done.

SETTING SMART GOALS

One of the first steps here is to define specific, measurable and realistic objectives according to your KPIs and current situation. Use the SMART concept for this:

S - Specific

M - Measurable

A - Achievable

R - Relevant

T - Thunderstorms

Examples applying the formula:

- Increase sales by 20% in the next 3 months

- Get 10 new weekly leads in 6 weeks

- Receive 30 5-star reviews in the next quarter

Having these goals very clear about what needs to change, it becomes more tangible to outline actions and - monitor this evolution by numbers over the defined time.

KPIs: your vital indicators

We've already talked a lot about the importance of defining key metrics that will be your guide to whether your actions are yielding results or not. Some of the main KPIs that you should consider in your planning:

- Online sales / monthly billing

- Number of new customers acquired

- Qualified leads or contacts collected

- Direct and organic traffic to your website

- Reach, engagement and followers on social media

- Visitor to sales conversion rate

- Cost per customer acquisition

Tools like Google Analytics, your email marketing tool, and social dashboards will give you these numbers. Compare with your objectives and goals.

SCHEDULING EXECUTION

Once you have closed your ideas, metrics and objectives, it's time to actually execute your digital marketing plan.

Map everything out on a schedule:

- Next 3 months (90 days)

- Divided into weeks

- With each determined initiative (e.g. post about X topic, setting up Facebook pixel, etc.)

- Defining responsible and status

This will guide your team and your own efforts to implement all aspects of the plan in an organized and focused manner.

Review this schedule weekly to assess your progress. If necessary, renegotiate deadlines or reorganize activities based on learning.

Always work with 90-day cycles in this planning. At the end of these cycles, deeply reevaluate your KPIs, objectives and action plan.

I hope that you now feel much more confident in putting into practice the digital marketing strategies taught throughout this book and, most importantly, doing so in the most structured way possible to achieve success with your ultimate online presence and sales goals.

Take this content forward, apply it in your specific context and let's dominate the digital environment together!

CONCLUSION AND MAP FOR APPLYING THE STRATEGIES LEARNED IN THE NEXT 90 DAYS, STARTING FROM TODAY: A DAY BY STEP STEP BY DAY FOR ENTREPRENEURS TO APPLY SIMPLE STRATEGIES

We have reached the last chapter of our journey to boost your digital presence!

Throughout the previous lessons, we learned dozens of strategies, techniques and insights about digital marketing with the aim of bringing more customers and sales to your business.

But how can we actually put all of this into practice in the coming months in a consistent, structured way that brings results?

In this final chapter, I created a step-by-step guide with daily actions for the next 90 days in order to practically apply **ALL** the teachings presented so far in their specific context.

This is a complete and motivational guide for you to achieve small victories day after day that add up until the dream digital transformation of your business becomes a reality!

Already ready to get your hands dirty? So let's go with everything!

WEEK 1 - FIRST STEPS

MONDAY

Objective: Define your success KPIs

Do some initial brainstorming and a mind map with all the possible indicators that can measure your business's online success in the coming months. Analyze each one and choose 5 to 7 essential KPIs that will be your digital "thermometer" to monitor whether things are on the right track.

Some suggestions: organic website traffic, number of followers on social media, online sales generated, number of new contacts collected, etc.

TUESDAY

Objective: Establish your goals

Next, quantify where you want to get to in a given period of time for each of these KPIs that you chose yesterday. Remember the

SMART concept: specific, measurable, achievable, relevant goals with a well-defined time limit.

Examples: increase website traffic by 30% in the next 90 days, gain 500 new leads in 2 months, etc. This will help you to be data-driven and have a realistic thermometer of your progress.

WEDNESDAY

Objective: Define your main buyer persona

Reflect and write down the typical demographic characteristics, behaviors, interests, and values of your current target audience or primary buyer persona. Consult data from your existing customers if necessary.

Include things like the most common age and gender, geographic location, most common job titles or area of expertise, what problem your product or service solves for them, and so on.

Defining your ideal client will help you direct all your next actions in a much more assertive way, speaking directly to them from now on.

THURSDAY

Objective: Research relevant keywords

Use Google Keyword Planner or other tools to discover the main keywords and terms searched by your target audience when they want to find or buy something related to your products or services.

Make a list of the 20 most relevant and least contested search words and phrases. You will need these terms to apply on several SEO fronts in the coming days.

FRIDAY

Objective: Define exclusive selling proposition

Think carefully and write down what your business's main

competitive advantage is. In other words, that special characteristic that makes you stand out from your competition in the eyes of the consumer.

This will be an important concept to convey in your content over the next few weeks and one that drives many of the strategies recommended in this book.

WEEK 2 - ON SITE OPTIMIZATION

MONDAY

Goal: Set up Google Analytics + other integrations

Install the Google Analytics tracking code on every page on your site if you haven't already. This tool is essential for extracting insights into your traffic. Also integrate other monitoring solutions like Facebook Pixel, online chat tools, and other useful features to keep track of visitors and leads.

TUESDAY

Purpose: Update website information

Check that all basic information on the website such as contact telephone numbers, physical store address, opening hours, institutional pages and others are correctly filled out. This avoids communication noise with your visitors.

WEDNESDAY

Objective: Optimize pages based on SEO

Choose at least 5 main pages on your website and invest a few hours optimizing the texts on these screens according to SEO guidelines. Include relevant keywords in the title, url , first paragraphs, use H1, H2 tags and internal links between content. This will boost your organic reach.

THURSDAY

Objective: Build lead magnets/capture pages

Create free content (e-books, lists, guides, spreadsheets) focused on your buyer persona and with themes that bring great value according to their pains and interests. Produce strategic pages to capture the data (name and email at a minimum) of those who download these materials in exchange. These leads will be important for many strategies in the coming days.

FRIDAY

Objective: Set up marketing automations

Map out where the main gaps and weaknesses are in your online sales funnel today and start designing marketing automation flows to address these issues. For example: Sending follow-up emails to anyone who downloads an ebook, alerts for abandoned carts, personalized recommendations, etc. There are several accessible tools to automatically create these journeys based on people's behavior. Search for Active Campaign , RD Station, Mailchimp , etc. Start implementing at least one flow this weekend.

WEEK 3 - PAID TRAFFIC

MONDAY

Objective: Define your monthly ad budget

Determine how much of your current revenue you can reinvest each month in paid campaigns. Remember that to achieve exponential growth, big brands invest 10 to 30% on average. But start where you can, the important thing is to start from scratch and optimize. For example, R$300 or R$500 per month already brings good results if well invested.

TUESDAY

Purpose: Set up Facebook pixel

Install the Facebook pixel on your website as soon as possible. This small fragment of code will allow us to track conversions that occurred through the campaigns and ads that we will run on this network, in addition to making it possible to create similar target audiences to scale even further.

WEDNESDAY

Objective: Create your Google Ads account

Create your account on the Google advertising platform. Start by familiarizing yourself with the interface and explore reach-focused campaign options like display ads and discovery ads . Don't forget to download Google Ads Editor to make management easier via desktop. Tomorrow we will actually launch our first ad there!

THURSDAY

Goal: Launch your first Facebook/Instagram ad

Create your first targeted paid campaign to attract more followers and engagement on social media. Focus on this initially, then we will generate traffic to your website and work with conversions. Explore ad formats within Facebook Business Manager, starting with response ads (call-to-action for likes, subscriptions, etc.). Set a low initial budget, something like R$15 or $20 per day to test.

FRIDAY

Purpose: Set up Google alerts

Within the Google Alerts tool, register keywords related to your business and some common spelling errors to receive an alert every time someone publishes something on the internet talking about your brand. This will help you monitor relevant conversations and your online reputation 24 hours a day.

WEEK 4 - EMAIL, RELATIONSHIPS AND REPUTATION

MONDAY

Objective: Create standardized landing page

Set up a standard "Thank You" page to display after conversions for important goals like list signups, purchases, and downloads. Visually structure it in line with your website pages and include instructions for next steps, such as checking the welcome email, for example.

This increases your credibility and retention rate of these newly acquired leads.

TUESDAY

Goal: Produce a series of useful posts

Create a list of at least 10 post ideas that you can share in the coming weeks, bringing insights and solutions to your buyer persona's common pain points and questions. The more useful and truly relevant to your audience, the more engagement it will bring.

WEDNESDAY

Purpose: Set up automatic welcome email

Within your email marketing and marketing automation platform, create a flow so that every new contact who signs up to your lists immediately receives an automated welcome email. Personalize with the contact's name, better present your brand and include an incentive for interaction.

THURSDAY

Purpose: Enable quick replies on Facebook/Instagram

Within the settings of your social media pages, enable the quick replies feature. This way, you can select pre-defined messages for certain common questions or requests that your audience sends, speeding up support. But don't leave it 100% automatic, cultivate relationships by also responding in a manual and personalized way whenever you can.

FRIDAY

Objective: Request reviews on public platforms

Your business probably already has some public reputation profiles, such as on Google, Facebook or review platforms. Today, actively ask your good customers to leave a 5-star review on these places. This goes a long way toward building authority and confidence for new potential customers.

WEEK 5 and 6 - CONTINUITY WITH A FOCUS ON THE LONG TERM

Now that we have implemented several fundamental initiatives, it is time to continue and start constantly thinking about new medium and long-term strategies, always looking at your KPIs and adjusting efforts accordingly.

Over the next 2 weeks, I recommend:

- Follow up on useful post ideas, turning them into a consistent editorial calendar.

- Invest an hour a day in producing new pages and content for your website.

- Create new paid campaigns with different objectives and audience segments.

- Join relevant Facebook and Reddit groups to interact with your buyer persona.

- Carry out incremental copy and creative tests in your online ads.

- Search on Google which sites talk about your company or have potential for future partnerships.

And so on. Keep your action plan in continuous execution, always looking for small improvements in both short-term efforts and initiatives that will only bring consistent results in the medium and long term.

Remember to celebrate every little victory too! It all adds up to keep you and your team motivated on this journey of exponential growth.

WEEK 7 - OPTIMIZATIONS AND NEW HORIZONS

The time has come for our first in-depth analysis to understand together what worked or not in this first cycle carried out over the last 7 weeks.

First, look at Google Analytics, Facebook Ads Manager and other monitoring solutions for the main results:

- Did your traffic, sales and leads increase? While?

- Which pages and channels performed best?

- Is engagement with your content growing?

- Compare everything to the goals we set in week 1. Celebrate the wins!

Then evaluate your digital presence critically. Some questions to help you:

- What problems does my audience still frequently face?

- How can I further improve people's experience with my brand?

- What new customer segment can we explore?

- What strategic partnerships should we start developing?

- How can we bring innovation and differentiate ourselves in this market?

Let new insights and testing ideas emerge. And define at least three growth challenges to address in the next 90-day cycle that begins.

You are on the right track. Keep it up!

WEEK 8 UNTIL THE END OF 90 DAYS - EXPONENTIAL GROWTH

Now, my friend, you have all the tools to reap the rewards of digital marketing and take your business to new heights in the coming months!

Continue implementing new initiatives, optimizing existing efforts and increasingly cultivating your relationship with the public.

The secrets to getting faster and faster are: consistency, discipline and organization. So keep your action plan in continuous motion, periodically analyzing what works or needs adjustments.

Celebrate every small victory and new customer gained. Evolve, innovate and adapt quickly to changes in your segment and consumer behavior.

I believe in your potential. Now, let's continue this journey together to the next level!

Take care of yourself and may your business prosper thanks to everything you learned here.

A big hug!

As we turn the final page of this journey together, I sincerely hope that the learnings shared here have touched your heart and sparked new perspectives. If this book has brought you any value, I kindly ask that you take a few moments to leave a review on Amazon. Your words not only help me grow and hone my craft, but they also guide other readers in their quests for knowledge and inspiration. Your opinion is a valuable gift, both for me and for the community of readers looking for stories that transform. I sincerely thank you for sharing this journey with me and I hope we can meet again in the pages of a new adventure.

REGINALDO OSNILDO

Hello, I'm Reginaldo Osnildo, author and innovator in the areas of sales, technology, and communication strategies. My experience ranges from the academic environment, as a professor and researcher at the University of Southern Santa Catarina, to practice as a strategist at Grupo Catarinense de Rádios. With a PhD in sales narratives and digital convergence, and a master's degree in storytelling and social imaginary, I bring my readers a unique fusion of theory and practice. My goal is to provide knowledge in a simple, practical and didactic language, encouraging direct application in personal and professional life.

Yours sincerely

Reginaldo Osnildo

+55 48 991913865

reginaldoosnildo@gmail.com